R.G.'s On Vacation

Written by Lisa L. Dwyer
Illustrated by Joanne Ferrante

Window Seat Publishing

Window Seat Publishing, Inc.
West Hempstead, NY

For Randolph George Brown Jr.
With Love, Ms. Lisa

For Phil and Andy – With love, JF

R.G.'s on vacation with his family.
They went down to the beach to look upon the sea.
And when they looked upon the sea,
they searched up and down.

ZERO friendly sea creatures were all that could be found!

R.G.'s on vacation with his family.
They went down to the beach to look upon the sea.
And when they looked upon the sea,
this is what they saw.

ONE solitary seal sitting by the shore!

R.G.'s on vacation with his family.
They went down to the beach
to look upon the sea.

And when they looked upon the sea,
this is what they spied.

TWO gorgeous angelfish
swimming side by side!

JF

R.G.'s on vacation with his family.
They went down to the beach to look upon the sea.
And when they looked upon the sea, this was what was there.

THREE graceful dolphins
flying through the air!

R.G.'s on vacation with his family.
They went down to the beach to look upon the sea.
And when they looked upon the sea, they had to hum along.

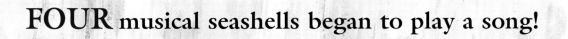

FOUR musical seashells began to play a song!

R.G.'s on vacation with his family.
They went down to the beach to look upon the sea.
And when they looked upon the sea, they got a great shock.

FIVE electric eels hopped up on the dock!

R.G.'s on vacation with his family.
They went down to the beach
to look upon the sea.

And when they looked upon the sea,
they saw to their surprise

SIX baby sea turtles opening their eyes!

R.G.'s on vacation with his family.
They went down to the beach to look upon the sea.
And when they looked upon the sea, they saw a funny sight.

SEVEN curious sea gulls
flying 'round a kite!

R.G.'s on vacation with his family.
They went down to the beach to look upon the sea.
And when they looked upon the sea, they really had to laugh.

EIGHT sunburned horseshoe crabs tried to take a bath!

R.G.'s on vacation with his family.
They went down to the beach
to look upon the sea.
And when they looked
upon the sea,
this is who they met.

NINE tired fishermen
pulling in their net!

R.G.'s on vacation with his family.
They went down to the beach to look upon the sea.
And when they looked upon the sea,
they laughed so hard they cried.

TEN silly sea horses were surfing in the tide!

R.G.'s on vacation with his family.
They went down to the beach to look upon the sea.
And when they looked upon the sea, much to their delight

ELEVEN happy starfish danced in the moonlight!

R.G.'s on vacation
They went down to the beach
And when they looked upon the sea

TWELVE sleepy lobsters put

with his family.
to look upon the sea.
they knew the day was done.

their heads down one by one!

THE

END

Published by:
Window Seat Publishing, Inc.
82 Marlborough Rd., Suite 108
West Hempstead, NY 11552
www.windowseatpublishing.com

ISBN: 0-9721949-1-6
LIBRARY OF CONGRESS CONTROL NUMBER: 2003101955

Printed in Hong Kong
Book Design: Budget Book Design
Printed by: BooksJustBooks.com

This is a  book.

Window Seat Publishing